MicroVictories

A Life of Celebration, Gratitude, and Purpose

Sean K. Brooks

Table of Contents

Dedication

For Melissa Savard, my loving angel.

Your love, light, and presence continue to guide me. In the quiet moments, in the strength I carry forward, and in every small victory, you remain with me.

This book is a reflection of the gratitude you helped cultivate in my life and the purpose your love gave me.

Forever loved. Forever missed. Forever part of my journey.

Preface: My Story

I discovered MicroVictories at a young age without ever giving them a label. In seventh grade, I was a lanky, four-eyed boy with nappy hair and bad breath because I hated brushing my teeth. For eighth grade, I transferred from a charter elementary school in the heart of North Philadelphia that required uniforms to a new-wave charter school for grades eight through twelve in Center City Philadelphia with no uniform requirements.

In my geography class, we played geography quiz games each week. We were permitted to form teams of up to six students. My friend Derek and I always chose a two-person team, and eventually nicknamed it $NERDZ^2$. We won almost every week, which infuriated the other students. I had a girlfriend, a social circle, and was considered a smart kid. I was funny and very athletic. One day, I realized, "Wow! I'm actually really awesome," and just like that, my self-love was born.

High school reinforced my self-worth. I was fortunate enough to attend an incredible private Catholic, all-boys, college-preparatory school. I was fully involved in sports, community service, and mentoring with teachers and staff who continuously encouraged me and facilitated my development.

I continued my education at an incredibly diverse and metropolitan university on the main campus in Jamaica, Queens, NY. I joined a fraternity and continued my academic career and mentorship.

After graduation, I moved across the country to Arizona, working in manufacturing for a range of companies in QA, QC, and Regulatory Affairs. I've always felt that my mentality was unique, especially for people in my field; however, I realized that I could share my mindset and help people while coaching and supporting friends, colleagues, and family members over the years.

I wrote these pages not as a novel or a one-time-use book, but as a coffee table, bathroom toilet, and nightstand reference manual. These are concepts and insights you can draw on at any moment in time, a book meant to be read and shared over and over again.

I first thought I had finished this book after becoming the victim of a hit-and-run. While riding my moped to physical therapy, I was blindsided by a minivan in a roundabout. The van sideswiped me, knocking me off my moped and onto the ground. The driver stopped and looked out his window.

With the help of a few good Samaritans who witnessed the accident, I sat up as they came to my aid. The driver looked directly at me, then sped off through the resort, running every stop sign until reaching the main road. I was fortunate enough to walk away with a torn medial meniscus, some bumps and bruises, and a newfound appreciation for life. With only liability insurance and no license plate number, the police and insurance company informed me there was nothing they could do to help.

The accident occurred just two weeks before a trip I had planned with my girlfriend to Colombia. I refused to allow this setback to break my spirit. But the world was not done with me yet. Just a few weeks after returning from vacation, I lost my job. Instead of being disappointed, I took the opportunity to refine the book, take training courses to expand my professional knowledge, and work on household projects.

After four weeks, I found a new job, and things were looking up. I believed I was living the book in real time. Then tragedy struck, and my life was forever changed. On August 29, 2025, I lost the love of my life, Melissa, in a tragic accident while camping in Northern Arizona. I felt lost and angry at the world. That was when I understood what this book was truly meant for. Suddenly, I needed it more than ever. I needed to live by my own words and my own philosophy.

Ever since that day, I take nothing for granted. Melissa believed in me. She believed in this book and in how these words could help people.

This book is dedicated to Melissa's life and legacy.

"This is the true joy in life: being used for a purpose recognized by yourself as a mighty one. Being a force of nature instead of a feverish, selfish little clod of ailments and grievances, complaining that the world will not devote itself to making you happy. I am of the opinion that my life belongs to the whole community, and as long as I live, it is my privilege to do for it what I can. I want to be thoroughly used up when I die, for the harder I work, the more I live. I rejoice in life for its own sake. Life is no brief candle to me. It is a sort of splendid torch which I have got hold of for the moment, and I want to make it burn as brightly as possible before handing it on to future generations."

– George Bernard Shaw

Note from the Author

When I first set out to write this book, I wanted it to be concise: short and to the point. I wanted to write something that expresses my views on relationships and human connection, and to share anecdotal stories to help illustrate my points.

As you read through each chapter, remember that these are real, true stories and situations that have influenced my mindset and helped me gain some insight into the behavior and relationships of those around me and connected to me.

Full Disclaimer: I am neither trained nor licensed in any therapeutic or counseling discipline. I have no formal education in psychology or sociology, apart from a few courses I took during my undergrad years at St. John's University. GO REDSTORM!

Introduction
Welcome to MicroVictories

This book is a culmination of a lifetime of gratitude. It's a testament to the friendships and relationships I've developed, the challenges I've faced, and the invaluable lessons I've learned along the way.

Over the years, I've realized that true fulfillment isn't found in grand achievements or distant dreams. It's found in the small victories, the quiet moments of progress, the connections with others, and the understanding that happiness is a choice we make daily.

Throughout this journey, I've learned that the way we approach life determines our experience. Gratitude, celebration, and purpose have been the pillars that've helped me navigate life's ups and downs with a sense of peace and fulfillment. This book isn't just a guide; it's a reflection on the path I've walked, one in which small steps, intentional choices, and a deep appreciation for the present moment have shaped the person I am today.

In these pages, you'll find practical insights, actionable steps, and personal reflections that have helped me grow. I hope that by sharing my journey, you too will be inspired to embrace the power of gratitude, purpose, and celebration in your own life.

The path ahead may not always be easy, but it will be worth it. Let's celebrate the small victories and appreciate the journey, knowing that it's not just the destination that matters, but the way we choose to live along the way.

Welcome to the journey. Welcome to your *MicroVictories.*

Chapter 1
Celebration: The Power of Small Wins

The Power of the *MicroVictory*: Rebalancing Your Day

One single negative moment, even something as minor as scuffing your new shoes on the way to a morning meeting, can cast a long shadow over your entire day. This one moment of frustration can bleed into your mood, coloring every conversation, task, and interaction that follows. It's a phenomenon that relationship researchers Drs. John and Julie Gottman studied and found that in stable, happy relationships, it takes a 5-to-1 ratio of positive interactions to outweigh a single negative interaction. This suggests that we must consciously counterbalance moments of tension with moments of warmth, appreciation, or humor to maintain positive momentum.

The same principle applies to your own emotional well-being throughout the day. One negative experience can tip the balance in your internal scale. But here's the trick: by intentionally stacking five small positive actions, or *MicroVictories*, you can restore equilibrium. Your emotional bank account isn't about robbing yourself of joy; it's about making small, consistent deposits, especially when you need them most.

Celebrate What No One Else Sees

We live in a world that over-glorifies grand gestures and massive accomplishments: the promotions, the house closings, the weddings. Yet, behind every giant win are countless small tasks, the everyday moments where you chose to move, act, and push forward when you didn't have to. These are the building blocks of a fulfilled life, and they deserve celebration.

A *MicroVictory* is not about finishing a marathon; it's about tying your shoes and stepping outside. It's not about writing a book in one sitting; it's about opening the document and typing that first sentence. These seemingly minor achievements are often invisible to the world, but they don't need an audience to matter. They are powerful because they show you're still moving, still trying, still investing in yourself. These small actions, when done with intention, compound over time. They build momentum, which builds confidence.

There is a unique joy in simply finishing something. We often overlook the satisfaction of checking a box or seeing a task through to completion. Even mundane chores, when done with purpose, give us a small, quiet satisfaction. Over time, these successes stack up, making you feel more capable, grounded, and confident. This is why celebration matters. It's not self-indulgence; it's self-recognition.

The Power of Small Celebrations as MicroVictories

Celebration doesn't always need to be grand or loud; it can be quiet, subtle, and deeply personal. A genuine smile is one way your body marks success, but so is a slow exhale after finishing a task, a nod of acknowledgment to yourself, or the simple act of closing your laptop with satisfaction. These are all small, intentional gestures that say, *"I did that. I showed up."*

A *MicroVictory* can take many forms: standing a little taller, stretching your arms wide after progress, taking a sip of coffee and really tasting it, or writing a quick "good job" note to yourself. These small celebrations honor your effort in real time.

Each one, whether it's a smile, a deep breath, or a quiet pause, anchors you in gratitude and presence. They become signals to yourself and to the world that you are aware, accomplished, and at peace, even in the smallest of ways.

Because waiting until something big happens is a trap. A lie. If you don't learn to recognize the beauty in the daily, you'll always chase fulfillment but never feel it.

Why Celebrate Small Wins?

Celebrating a small win isn't about being proud of mediocrity. It's about anchoring yourself in progress. About saying to yourself, *"I showed up today. I did something today. I moved."*

That's where confidence is built, not in giant leaps, but in the compound effect of little wins.

Every day presents opportunities for small victories. Waking up with intention. Making yourself breakfast. Texting a friend to check in. Choosing to take the stairs. Speaking up. Taking a breath instead of reacting. Smiling at a stranger. Drinking more water. Saying thank you and meaning it.

These aren't just habits or chores. They are choices. And when made with awareness and gratitude, they are *MicroVictories* — the building blocks of a meaningful life.

Happiness isn't a finish line you cross; it's a rhythm you dance to every single day. And that rhythm? It's built from small, deliberate, joyful steps. Steps we often overlook. But that's where the real magic is.Don't breeze past your efforts. Celebrate them.

Remember To Celebrate Yourself

Light a candle when you complete your task list. Write down

three wins at the end of each day. Say out loud what you're proud of. Dance a little. Smile a lot. Acknowledge the you that made the hard choices, even when no one was watching.

And most importantly, thank yourself. Thank yourself for showing up for your life.

Action Step:

Tonight, before bed, ask yourself:

- *What did I do today that I'm proud of?*

- *Where did I show up even when I didn't have to?*

- *What small victory am I carrying into tomorrow?*

Write it down. Feel it. Own it.

Because those wins? That's the life you're building. And it's worth celebrating.

Choose one small task. It could be as simple as folding the laundry, drinking a full glass of water, or making your bed. Complete it with full awareness and intention. Then, smile, not for anyone else, but for you.

That's a *MicroVictory*. And tomorrow, do it again.

Chapter 2
Gratitude: The Art of Presence

Gratitude is not about grand gestures. It's not about elaborate thank-you cards or public declarations. Gratitude is simply presence, the act of noticing, appreciating, and honoring the moment you're in and the people you share it with.

In today's world, it's easy to live distracted. Our minds jump between screens, tasks, and worries. We think about tomorrow's deadlines or yesterday's mistakes. We rarely sit in the now. But real gratitude requires us to do just that.

Be Present. Be Intentional

When you're in a conversation, make the words of the person in front of you matter. Listen, not just to respond, but to *understand*. Show interest, but be genuine. Connect with their words. Listen with intention.

There's an energy exchange when we are fully present with another person. They feel seen, valued, and important. That's gratitude in motion.

In many of my social circles, I've been seen as a safe haven. Someone people could call when they were in trouble — stranded, drunk, assaulted, or just in need of a ride. They knew I'd answer. That reliability is not just kindness; it's gratitude for the relationship itself, expressed through action.

Look for the Positive

Gratitude is also about mindset. I once heard a story about a man who hated long lines. One day, he met a Japanese man who told him that in Japan, people love queues. Why? Because a long line means there's something worthwhile at the end. Instead of focusing on inconvenience, they focus on anticipation.

That's gratitude — choosing to frame situations in a way that highlights potential and positivity.

Useful, Not Dependent

The more useful you are to your community, the more love and appreciation you feel. This isn't about creating dependency or martyrdom. It's about contributing because it's who you are. Being helpful without obligation, because you find joy in lightening someone else's load.

Different religions argue the divinity of Jesus. But for all their disagreement, there's no denying that Jesus was a real man, human in all those aspects that we use to define humanity. Jesus was conscientious, compassionate, and kind. He was a prophet. He served. He was of use. Muhammad, in the same light, was a prophet. Abraham, Muhammad, Moses, and Jesus are the most prominent prophets in Western religions. Siddhartha Gautama, Lao Tzu, and Confucius – prophets of Eastern religions and philosophies. Mother Theresa, Greta Thunberg, Nelson Mandela, Malala Yousafzai, and MLK – all prophets; outspoken community leaders who lead by example. Applying a secular definition of the term *'prophet'* allows for a more inclusive and pervasive evaluation and application of their philosophies. They offered healing, wisdom, and hope — not for personal gain, but because they found purpose in it. We can embody the same principle in our lives.

There is a balance: usefulness has limits. It's accepting *inconvenience*, not *abuse*. It's finding pleasure in knowing you've made someone's life easier, doing the right thing even when it was hard, telling the truth when it was difficult, and remaining true to yourself— and that small service is, in itself, a *MicroVictory*.

Action Step

Today, be fully present in one interaction. Listen with intention. Show up for someone, even in a small way. Acknowledge their words, their presence. Let them feel seen.

That's gratitude. That's a *MicroVictory*

Chapter 3
Purpose: Finding Your Way

Purpose is not something you stumble upon once in a lifetime. It's something you cultivate, question, return to, and redefine again and again. It's the inner compass that keeps you steady when life's storms shake your footing. And when you live with purpose, even the most mundane moments feel infused with meaning.

But how do you find your purpose?

The truth is, you already have it. It's just buried beneath expectations, distractions, and fear. You uncover it not by reaching outward, but by looking inward and paying attention to your curiosities, your strengths, your pain, and your joy.

The Japanese Principle of Ikigai

In Japanese culture, there's a beautiful concept called *ikigai* (生き甲斐), which translates to *"a reason for being."* Ikigai is the intersection of four elements:

- What you love

- What you're good at

- What the world needs

- What you can be paid for

Imagine each as a circle, and where all four overlap is your ikigai—your purpose. It's not just about doing something meaningful. It's about doing something sustainable, joyful, and useful.

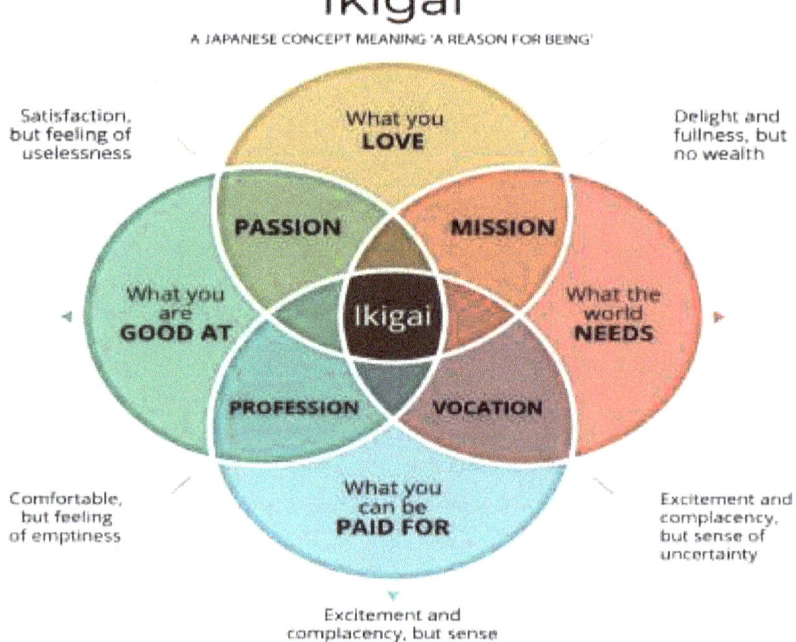

You don't need to fully satisfy all four areas overnight. Most of us start with one or two and grow into the others. But the goal is alignment—a life that feels coherent, where your actions echo your values.

Step One: What You Love

Ask yourself:

- *What do I do that makes me lose track of time?*

- *What topics could I talk about endlessly?*

- *What types of problems am I excited to solve?*

These questions lead you toward your passions. Don't worry if your answers seem impractical or scattered. This is where your energy lives.

Step Two: What You're Good At

Your talents, skills, and natural strengths matter. But this also includes what you're willing to work hard to become good at. Passion without practice is potential wasted. Purpose needs both.

Ask yourself:

- *What do others often come to me for?*

- *What skills do I enjoy sharpening?*

- *What have I always picked up quickly?*

Step Three: What the World Needs

Purpose expands when you connect it to others. This doesn't mean you need to save the world. It means contributing in ways that create value or joy for someone besides yourself.

Ask yourself:

- *Where do people need help that I can provide?*

- *What breaks my heart?*

- *What change do I wish to see?*

Step Four: What You Can Be Paid For

This is the bridge between passion and sustainability. Ikigai isn't about martyrdom. If your calling also supports you financially, it gives you the freedom to serve without burning out.

Ask:

- *What services or knowledge do I have that others find valuable?*

- *Is there a way to monetize my interests without selling out my values?*

- *Can I start small and grow?*

Let Purpose Evolve

Ikigai is not a static destination. It shifts as you grow. Your values may evolve. Your skills may deepen. Your priorities may change. That's not failure. That's growth.

You might start your journey by teaching kids to play basketball and later become a coach, therapist, or author. The deeper thread—supporting growth, inspiring resilience—remains. Throughout my life, I've served in many positions and roles: camp counselor, lifeguard and swim instructor, campus security, pledge educator and master, grandmaster of ceremonies, kickball team captain, quality manager, and director. I've always been drawn to positions where I work with people, educating them academically and socially, and providing security and guidance.

Sometimes, purpose isn't a job title or a mission statement. Sometimes, it's a pattern. A recurring instinct to show up in a certain way. A consistent joy in a certain activity. That is your compass.

The Role of Purpose in Health and Well-being

In Okinawa, Japan—one of the world's original Blue Zones—the concept of *ikigai* plays a defining role in the residents' longevity and well-being. Purpose is not an abstract idea, but a guiding principle embedded in daily life, influencing how people eat, move, and connect with others.

While not a traditional Blue Zone formed through centuries of culture, Singapore has emerged as a "Blue Zone 2.0," according to Dan Buettner, where longevity is engineered through intentional policies and community design. The nation's approach demonstrates that health and purpose can be cultivated through modern infrastructure: accessible public transportation, fresh food availability, and preventive healthcare all support a longer, more fulfilling life. Beyond its systems, Singapore fosters *ikigai*-like purpose through civic engagement, volunteerism, and lifelong learning, offering citizens multiple avenues to find meaning and belonging.

Purpose as a Path to Longevity

Across every Blue Zone—whether in Singapore, Sardinia, or among the Seventh-day Adventists in Loma Linda—purpose acts as a quiet but powerful thread that binds long-lived communities together.

In Sardinia, purpose is rooted in family, tradition, and the daily rhythm of contribution—shepherds, artisans, and elders rise each day with a sense of usefulness and connection. Among Adventists, purpose takes on a spiritual form, grounded in service, faith, and the belief that caring for others honors their divine mission.

Singapore's modern model mirrors these values through balance and contribution—citizens find purpose in community participation, social responsibility, and lifelong growth.

Across these diverse regions, purpose transcends culture and geography. It is not a lofty ideal but a lived practice, shaping identity, guiding action, and ultimately sustaining both health and life itself.

Purpose Is Direction, Not Pressure

Don't let the search for purpose become a source of stress. You don't need to have it all figured out. You just need to be willing to pay attention to what matters most to you and take action accordingly. The path will become clearer as you walk it. You're not "behind" in life if you haven't found your purpose. You're living in process. And every small act of alignment, every *MicroVictory* that resonates with your values, is a step toward your ikigai. Purpose is essential for overall health and well-being, providing direction rather than pressure.

Action Step: Create Your Ikigai Map

Draw four overlapping circles and label them:

- What I Love

- What I'm Good At

- What the World Needs

- What I Can Be Paid For

List at least three things in each circle. Notice where they intersect. Then reflect:

- *What role can I create or evolve that honors these intersections?*

- *What is one small step I can take this week to align closer to that overlap?*

It could be volunteering. Taking a class. Starting a side hustle. Mentoring someone. Creating something. Expressing something.

Purpose isn't about magnitude. It's about meaning.

Live with it. Lead with it. Let it shift. Let it stretch. Just never stop listening to it.

That's how you live a life of intention. That's how you discover your why. That's how you build a *MicroVictory*.

Chapter 4
Relationships: The Currency of Connection

Celebration, gratitude, and purpose mean little if we live isolated from others. Relationships are the space where these pillars breathe life. Human connection — real connection — is the richest currency we have.

Let's be clear: relationships are reciprocal. Every relationship, whether with a friend, a partner, a colleague, or even a pet, involves a give-and-take. The best relationships are not perfectly balanced every second, but over time, they develop a rhythm. A mutual exchange of time, energy, kindness, and effort. Relationships thrive when both parties invest, contribute, and benefit.

The Reciprocal Nature of Relationships

Every relationship involves a transaction, an exchange of giving and getting. While the word "transaction" can sound cold, it simply describes this natural flow of reciprocity. From our connection to technology, where we pay for a service and receive a product or entertainment, to our bonds with animals and children, where we provide care and receive love and appreciation, this exchange is a fundamental part of all relationships. The nature of these transactions can be complex, like finding gratitude in a friend finally opening up about their struggles, or as simple as the happiness you feel when someone enjoys a meal you've cooked.

Friendship operates on the same principle. You invest time and energy by showing up, listening, helping, and caring. In return, you receive companionship, support, and love. This reciprocal effort is what allows a relationship to flourish. When both people act with deliberate intention and gratitude, the bond strengthens, and both individuals benefit from the deep rewards of laughter, support, and personal growth.

Healthy relationships are built on this balanced exchange. It's not about keeping a score, but understanding that both parties contribute to a shared connection. This mutual giving and receiving is what sustains and enriches our bonds, ensuring that the effort we put in is met with the benefits we value.

Compartmentalize Wisely

We often lump human relationships into broad categories: family and friends. But those are too vague. It's more helpful to compartmentalize:

- Friends, associates, and acquaintances

- Family, relatives

Friends, Acquaintances, and Associates

Friends are those you have personal relationships with. There's an intimacy in friendship that requires an emotional connection: mutual trust, shared experiences, and reliable support. You can be vulnerable with them. The truest and most intimate friendships can feel like family, often filling a void and being considered family members when communicating the depth to outsiders.

Associates are people you interact with because of shared goals, projects, or environments — like colleagues, club members, or neighbors. The relationship is purposeful but not necessarily personal. Enough that you can converse about common interests and be present at the same functions. Associates typically share friends but are not close enough to be friends themselves.

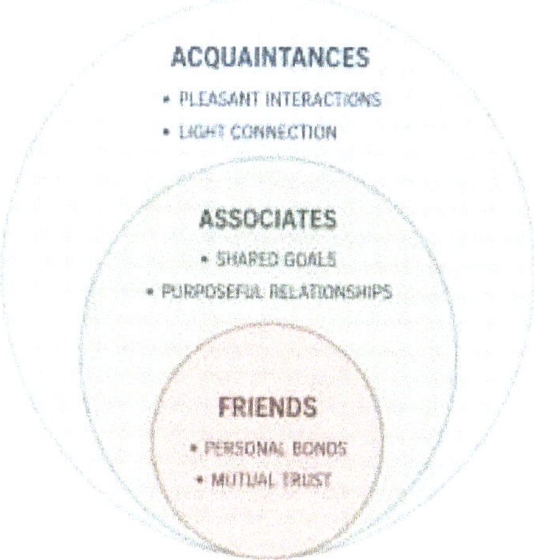

Acquaintances are people you know of, and may speak to in passing. Typically, associates share the same acquaintances and/or friends but are not directly connected to each other. The edges of social circles are connected by work, not by real personal connections. For example, Bob from accounting, Lisa who lives in the apartment down the hall, and the family you run into sometimes at the dog park. Acquaintances are people you enjoy casually, but without deep emotional investment. You see them occasionally, and interaction is pleasant but light.

Family vs. Relatives

Family is the people (and living beings like pets) with whom you have the most intimate connections. They rely on you, and you rely on them. These relationships give the most joy, but also cause the most sorrow. The emotional attachments to family are what make the relationships so important. Family can become friends when social interests are deeply shared. They are the people (related by blood or not) who uplift, respect, and cherish you. They show up, listen, and offer reciprocal love.

Relatives are those who are connected by blood or by law. An aunt or cousin, sibling or grandparent, parent or child, in-laws, and married partners. The key difference is the lack of emotional connection, shared interests, and/or values. Relatives are people you share genetics or legal ties with — but that does not automatically make them healthy, safe, or emotionally close. Not all blood ties are bonds of love, support, and trust. I tell people all the time that I have a small family with a lot of relatives.

Not everyone deserves the same access to you, and that's okay. Knowing who fits where allows you to invest your energy wisely. Pour deeply into your core circle — those who reciprocate, those who care for you as you care for them. Be vulnerable and grow with your family and friends. Show courtesy and kindness to acquaintances, associates, and relatives, but protect your emotional reserves.

The Tree of Connection

Think of relationships like a tree. Every person plays a role in the growth, stability, and vitality of the social ecosystem. Some people are the **trunks**—the deeply social connectors. They are the planners, the event organizers, the ones who hold the circle together. When you think of who brings people together for birthdays, dinners, or group trips, it's usually the trunks. The social network is rooted in them because they provide structure and consistency, giving the group a central foundation.

Most people, however, are **branches**. Branches don't always take on the responsibility of organizing, but they extend the network outward. They connect with others, strengthen bonds, and sometimes introduce new members into the circle when they sense the fit is right. Branches add reach and variety, giving the social tree its shape and helping relationships expand naturally.

Then there are the **leaves**. Leaves are the people on the edges of the circle. They show up when invited, they enjoy the connection, and they contribute energy and joy in their own way. But they are less likely to introduce new members or initiate gatherings themselves. Their presence is still essential—just as a tree without leaves would feel lifeless, a social circle without these participants would lack vibrancy and fullness.

Personally, I've held multiple roles. In some social circles, I've been the trunk—the one people counted on to bring everyone together. In others, I've been a branch, extending connections but not necessarily carrying the weight of organizing. Neither role is better; both matter. Each role has value. The trunk provides stability, the branches extend possibilities, and the leaves bring color and life.

When you recognize where you naturally fall in this metaphor, you can better understand your contribution to the health of your social ecosystem. More importantly, you learn to value the roles of others without judgment. A thriving tree requires every part to play its role. A thriving community is no different.

The Dangers of Isolation and the Power of Connection

Social isolation can have a profound negative impact on our overall health. Loneliness, which stems from a lack of connection, often leads to unhealthy habits and increased stress. Research has underscored the severity of this issue, with a 2019 study led by Kassandra Alcaraz of the American Cancer Society finding that social isolation increases the risk of premature death across all racial groups.

The risk associated with social isolation is comparable to other major health concerns. Alcaraz stated, *"Our research really shows that the magnitude of risk presented by social isolation is very similar in magnitude to that of obesity, smoking, lack of access to care, and physical inactivity."* This highlights how crucial social connections are for our well-being and longevity.

Beyond the risk of premature death, social isolation has a wide range of negative health consequences. A review co-authored by Louise C. Hawkley found that the feeling of being socially isolated can harm an individual's physical, mental, and cognitive health at every stage of life. The study links it to depression, poor sleep, impaired cognitive function, and issues with cardiovascular and immune systems, underscoring the serious toll that social disconnection can take.

Travel. See the world. Meet new people. Immerse yourself in different cultures, landscapes, and perspectives. Isolation shrinks you. Connection expands you.

Action Step

Today, reach out to someone you care about — a friend, a relative, an associate, an acquaintance — and offer a genuine compliment, a word of encouragement, or simply a check-in. Water that relationship. Nourish it and watch it grow.

That's connection. That's a *MicroVictory*.

Chapter 5
Dressing as Self-Expression: Wearing Your Story

Every morning, you stand before a closet and make a choice. At first glance, it might look like a simple decision about fabric and color. But if you look more closely, you'll see something deeper: the chance to express who you are before you say a single word.

Clothing is a language. The textures, shapes, colors, and combinations we choose become part of how we tell our story to the world and how we remind ourselves of that story throughout the day. Dressing for self-expression is not about trends or rules; it's about aligning the outside with the inside. It's about asking: *What am I communicating today, and how can I do that authentically?*

This chapter explores three ways to think about self-expression through clothing: dressing with intention, authenticity, and playfulness.

Section 1 – Dressing with Intention

Clothes can do more than cover our bodies; they can help us step into the mindset we want to inhabit. When you dress with intention, you're not just picking what looks "acceptable." You're choosing pieces that reflect how you want to feel and what you want to project.

Think of clothing as a form of energy setting. A crisp blazer might help you feel sharp and focused during an important meeting. A flowing dress might make you feel freer and more creative. Sneakers might invite movement and spontaneity. Every choice is a small but powerful ritual.

The key is not to overcomplicate it. You don't need a designer wardrobe or dozens of outfits. What matters is pausing long enough to ask: *What do I want to embody today? Confidence? Comfort? Curiosity?* Your answer can guide your outfit in subtle but meaningful ways.

Try this: Before getting dressed tomorrow, set an intention: *Today, I want to feel ___.* Choose at least one piece of clothing or an accessory that embodies that quality. Notice how wearing it shifts the way you carry yourself.

Section 2 – Dressing with Authenticity

For many of us, clothing choices are influenced by outside expectations—what's considered "appropriate," "attractive," or "professional." While those guidelines have their place, they can also drown out our inner voice. Dressing with authenticity means honoring your true tastes and preferences, even if they don't align with what everyone else is wearing.

Ask yourself: *What kinds of clothes make me feel most like myself?* Maybe it's bold colors that match your outgoing personality. Maybe it's simple, neutral pieces that let your calm nature shine through. Maybe it's mixing vintage finds with modern cuts, or wearing jewelry that carries family history.

Authenticity in dress is also about comfort, not just physical, but emotional. If an outfit makes you feel like you're wearing someone else's skin, it's a clue that it doesn't belong in your rotation. Clothing should support your self-expression, not stifle it.

Try this: Do a five-minute closet scan. Pull out three items that you absolutely love wearing—the ones that make you light up inside. Ask yourself what they have in common (color, cut, mood). This pattern is a clue to your authentic style.

Section 3 – Dressing with Playfulness

Self-expression doesn't have to be heavy or serious. Clothing can be a form of play, a way to explore different sides of yourself. Some days you may feel like leaning into minimalism; other days you might want to experiment with patterns, accessories, or bold shoes.

Playfulness is not about perfection; it's about curiosity. It's allowing yourself to try a scarf in a new way, mix unexpected colors, or wear something that makes you smile even if no one else "gets it." Clothing becomes a reminder that life isn't only about fitting in; it's about exploration and joy.

When you allow yourself to play, you expand your self-expression beyond the safe and familiar. And sometimes, those experiments lead to breakthroughs. You discover a new color you love, a silhouette that feels empowering, or a playful detail that becomes part of your signature look.

Try this: Once this week, add one playful element to your outfit—something small that makes you feel lighter, braver, or more creative. It could be a bright pair of socks, a vintage pin, or a bold lipstick. Notice how it changes your mood throughout the day.

Action Step – The Style Journal Exercise

For the next seven days, keep a mini style journal. Each morning:

1. Write one word that describes how you want to feel.

2. Choose an outfit or detail that reflects that intention.

3. In the evening, reflect: *Did your clothing support your self-expression? Did it shift your mood, or how others interacted with*

you?

By the end of the week, you'll notice patterns. Certain colors, textures, or pieces may consistently bring out your confidence, creativity, or calm. That's not coincidental; that's your authentic style speaking.

Clothing may not define who you are, but it can remind you of who you are becoming. Dressing with intention, authenticity, and playfulness allows you to step into each day as a living expression of your values and spirit.

And when you put on something that makes you feel more you, that's alignment. That's joy. That's a *MicroVictory*.

Chapter 6
Be of Service: The Joy of Usefulness

One of the most profound *MicroVictories* is discovering how meaningful it feels to be useful, not in a way that drains you, but in a way that uplifts your community and enriches your own sense of purpose. Usefulness is one of the quietest but most powerful ways to feel love, appreciation, and belonging. It is not about dependency; it's about a voluntary contribution that stems from who you are. The people who are most valued in their communities, friendships, and families are the ones who consistently bring something to the table, whether it's skills, compassion, effort, or simply their presence.

The Power of Contribution, Not Obligation

There's an important distinction between being useful and being selfless. Selflessness often implies a sacrifice to the point of depletion or even abuse. It can lead to burnout, resentment, and a feeling of being taken for granted. Usefulness, on the other hand, has healthy limits. It's about accepting an occasional inconvenience for the genuine pleasure of helping someone else. When you are useful, you are empowered, not drained. You are making a conscious choice to contribute because it aligns with your values and brings you a sense of purpose. This is a gift you offer freely, without the weight of obligation.

For centuries, people have found inspiration in figures who made service their life's work. Think of a man like Jesus; his life centered around service. He offered guidance, healing, and compassion not because he was obligated, but because he wanted to uplift others. His actions were a testament to the idea that true service is rooted in a desire to help, not in a mandate.

Be of Service Without Expectation

When you help others, resist the urge to tally favors or expect immediate reciprocation. Your usefulness is a gift, and the best gifts are given freely, without strings attached. Trust that the value you provide will ripple outward and return to you in due time. The greatest joy in service comes from the act itself, from easing someone's burden and expressing who you are. This is a powerful *MicroVictory* that builds your sense of purpose and connection to the world around you.

Finding Your Ways to Be Useful

Being of service doesn't have to involve grand gestures. It's often found in the small, everyday acts that make a big difference. Your usefulness is your gift, and you have many ways to share it:

- *Offer a hand:* Help a neighbor carry grocery, or assist a colleague struggling with a project.

- *Be a resource:* Offer advice or share a skill you possess.

- *Give your time:* Volunteer for a cause you care about or simply be present for someone who needs to talk.

- *Share a smile:* Even a simple smile can be a powerful form of service. It can be an invitation that welcomes connection and ease, or a show of strength and resolve. It's a non-verbal expression of peace and contentment that can uplift those around you.

These small acts of contribution compound and shape the story of your life. One of my favorite films, *Big Fish (2003)*, tells the story of a son who tries to understand his dying father by reliving the fantastical myths his father talked about his life. The film's conclusion, where the son meets all the people from his father's stories—now less mythical, but still deeply impacted by his father's life—powerfully illustrates how a life of adventure, challenge, and service to others creates a lasting legacy of connection and appreciation. The big fish symbolize the father's desire for profound personal growth, but his true legacy is the community he built through being of service.

The Importance of Setting Boundaries

Being useful does not mean saying yes to everything. Healthy usefulness is about knowing your limits and communicating them clearly. You can be a helpful, contributing member of your community and still honor your own needs for rest, time, and well-being. Saying "no" when you're at capacity isn't selfish; it's a necessary boundary that prevents burnout and ensures your contributions are sustainable and joyful. A truly useful person is not a martyr but a well-balanced individual who understands that their own well-being is essential to their ability to help others effectively.

Action Step: The Smile as Service

Today, find one way to be useful to someone, whether by offering a hand, giving advice, or simply sharing a smile. Do it intentionally, with joy. Notice the feeling you get from making a positive difference in someone's day.

That's contribution. That's a *MicroVictory*.

Chapter 7
Intention: The Power Behind Every Action

If there's a single principle that amplifies all others in this book, it's intention. Intention turns the smallest task into something meaningful. It's what separates an empty routine from a purposeful ritual. It's what transforms autopilot into conscious living.

Most of us glide through our days performing hundreds of tasks on autopilot. We brush our teeth, scroll our phones, answer emails, and cook meals — all with minimal awareness. The first step toward celebration is to slow down and pay attention. Put effort into performing a task with a purpose beyond just completing it.

For example, when you cook dinner tonight, don't just "get it over with." There's no shame in that; it's human nature. But here's the truth: intention changes everything. Think about nourishing your body. Think about the flavors, the smells, the effort it takes to chop and stir. Let that small act be something worthy of acknowledgment. Each step of the process brings you closer to a whole dish, a meal you prepared with your own two hands.

You'll be amazed at how many daily tasks are completed unconsciously and how much more fulfilled you feel when you bring awareness to them.

Do With Purpose, Not Just Completion

When you approach each task with intention, even something as small as washing a dish or sending a text, you infuse it with purpose beyond mere completion. You become aware of why you're doing it, who it benefits, and how it contributes to your broader sense of fulfillment.

Folding laundry isn't just folding laundry; it's preparing clean clothes that give you comfort and confidence. Sending a message isn't just communication; it's strengthening a relationship. Making your bed isn't a chore; it's setting the tone for an orderly, peaceful day.

Small Tasks Compound into Happiness

Every time you complete a small task with intention, you achieve a *MicroVictory*. These small wins stack up, compounding into a greater sense of control, contentment, and happiness. The ultimate form of control is creating your own happiness by your own accord, through your own actions.

"You are the captain of your own ship; don't let anyone else take the wheel."

– Michael Josephson

Ask Yourself the Key Question:

Is there one small action I can do right now to make this situation more enjoyable or less unpleasant for myself? If the answer is yes, do that thing, regardless of whose fault the situation is, or whether you "should have to." The goal is a better outcome for **you**. That's self-care. That's wisdom.

Presence Follows Intention

When you act with intention, you naturally become more present. Your awareness sharpens. You listen better. You notice details. You connect more deeply with people, tasks, and even yourself. Intention is what turns life from a blur into something vivid and rich.

MicroVictories

Action Step

Today, choose one routine task, something you usually do on autopilot, and perform it with full intention. Pay attention to every step. Reflect on how it makes your life better.

That's intention. That's a *MicroVictory*.

Chapter 8
The Quiet Mirror: Practicing Introspection Anywhere

Introspection is not a luxury; it's a necessity. We live in a world that rewards speed, noise, and constant connection, yet the deepest insights about who we are rarely arrive in the middle of a rush. They come in the spaces between the doing, when we stop long enough to notice what's happening inside.

You don't have to book a silent retreat in the mountains to practice introspection. You don't even need to be sitting cross-legged on a cushion (though that's great, too). Introspection can be as simple as turning your attention inward while walking through a park, brushing your teeth, or driving home with the radio low. What matters is not the environment; it's the willingness to meet yourself there with intention, gratitude, and presence.

This chapter explores three ways to approach introspection: cultivating awareness in motion, creating space in stillness, and asking questions that open doors instead of closing them.

Awareness in Motion

Many people think reflection only happens when you're still, but movement can be just as fertile a ground for self-discovery. When the body moves in a steady rhythm, the mind often loosens its grip on the to-do list, making space for deeper thought.

Think of the times you've solved a problem while taking a shower, had an "aha!" moment during a long drive, or felt clarity walking down a familiar path. These aren't coincidences. Rhythmic, low-effort activities create a subtle meditative state in which insights can surface.

When you practice awareness in motion, your attention becomes anchored in the present moment. You notice the way your feet meet the ground, the sound of leaves brushing in the wind, the way sunlight spills across your path. This is presence, not as a concept, but as an experience. And when you're present, gratitude has room to bloom. You begin to see beauty in what's ordinary: the hum of the engine, the warmth of your hands, the rhythm of your own breath.

Try this: Next time you're walking, driving, or doing something repetitive, set an intention before you start: *I will be present with what arises.* As you move, silently name one thing you're grateful for in that moment. Let that feeling settle in your body. If a memory surfaces, let it play out. If an idea appears, turn it over in your mind like a stone in your hand.

Creating Space in Stillness

Stillness is the traditional home of introspection for a reason. When you unplug from external input—no screens, no conversation, no music—your mind's background noise becomes audible. At first, it might be messy: worries, replayed conversations, random thoughts about groceries. But if you stay with it, that surface static gives way to deeper currents.

Stillness doesn't have to mean sitting perfectly still in complete silence (though that can be powerful). It can also mean lying on the floor with your eyes closed, watching the clouds from a park bench, or sitting at your kitchen table with a cup of tea and nothing else.

When you enter stillness, set an intention to listen without judgment. This prevents the mind from slipping into self-criticism and keeps the door open to discovery. Presence is your compass. When you notice yourself drifting into past regrets or future worries, gently bring your focus back to your breath or your surroundings.

Gratitude can be the bridge between distraction and presence. If your thoughts scatter, name something in your current environment you're thankful for—the weight of the chair supporting you, the sound of rain outside, the fact that you have ten minutes to yourself. Gratitude anchors you in the now.

Try this: Set a timer for ten minutes. Sit or lie somewhere comfortable, close your eyes if you like, and watch your thoughts. Imagine you're sitting by a stream, and each thought is a leaf drifting past. When the timer ends, write down one thing you learned about yourself and one thing you're grateful for from the experience.

Asking the Right Questions

Introspection without curiosity is just rumination. If you only replay the same events or thoughts without digging deeper, you risk reinforcing old stories instead of discovering new truths. The tool that turns reflection into growth is the question.

The right question opens a door. The wrong one slams it shut. For example:

- *"Why am I such a failure?"* is a closed, self-punishing question—it invites only shame.

- *"What can I learn from this setback?"* is open and forward-looking—it invites possibility.

Questions become even more powerful when they're paired with intention, gratitude, and presence.

Intention guides the question: *What truth am I seeking right now?*

Gratitude keeps the exploration kind: *What part of my journey am I thankful for, even if it's hard?*

Presence keeps it real: *What am I feeling in this exact moment, without editing?*

Try this: Choose one open-ended question and carry it with you for a day. Let it simmer while you walk, cook, commute, or sit in stillness. Resist the urge to force an answer. Often, your subconscious will work on the question in the background, and the answer will appear unexpectedly, sometimes in the middle of rinsing dishes or stepping out of the shower.

When you combine introspection with intention, gratitude, and presence, you create a space where your inner life can breathe. You stop being a stranger to yourself and start becoming an ally.

The beauty of introspection is that it can happen anywhere— in the middle of a forest, in the front seat of your car, or while wiping down the kitchen counter. What matters most is not the setting, but the willingness to turn inward, listen, and respond with kindness.

Action Step – The Seven-Day Introspection Practice

For the next seven days, dedicate at least fifteen minutes to intentional introspection, weaving in gratitude and presence each time. Rotate through these three modes:

Day 1 & 4 – *Awareness in Motion:* Walk, drive, or do a repetitive task in silence. Before starting, set an intention. During, notice your surroundings and name at least one thing you're grateful for.

Day 2 & 5 – *Stillness:* Sit quietly with no distractions. Hold the intention to listen without judgment. When your mind wanders, anchor yourself in something you appreciate about the moment.

Day 3 & 6 – *Questions:* Pick one open-ended question to guide the day. Stay present to what arises and practice gratitude for any insight, no matter how small.

Day 7 – *Integration:* Review the week's notes. Look for patterns, recurring themes, or surprising insights. Acknowledge yourself with gratitude for showing up.

That's self-awareness. That's a *MicroVictory*

Chapter 9
The Power of Duality:
Embracing All of Who You Are

We are complex beings, full of layers and identities that don't always fit into neat boxes. One of life's greatest *MicroVictories* is learning to embrace your own **duality**—balancing the different facets of who you are and flowing effortlessly between them. Duality is key to this process. You can carry both masculine and feminine energies; you can be soft and strong, compassionate and assertive, and introspective and outgoing. True fulfillment comes not from choosing one side, but from integrating all of who you are. This is about being dynamic, containing multitudes, and honoring every part of your identity.

I've lived this balance myself. I can spend a day dancing, crafting, and chatting with my girlfriends, fully present, relaxed, and joyful. Later, I can head to the game and the bar with the guys—engaged, excited, and fully immersed. I also regularly explore art galleries and go to restaurants and movies alone.

In all these situations, my authentic presence is felt. Both groups know they are accepted and valued by me without judgment. I enjoy being present without companionship because I am comfortable and confident in each space. When you allow yourself to flow naturally among these different aspects of your identity, you become a safe space for others to be themselves without the pressure to perform a role. You become the person who listens deeply, offers advice when asked, and welcomes others as they are.

Integrate, Don't Separate

Our culture often tries to force us into rigid, either/or categories—masculine or feminine, logical or emotional, serious or playful. This rigid thinking is a **binary**, which is often easier for people to comprehend, but it fails to capture the complexity of human identity. True fulfillment comes when you embrace the dynamic, multifaceted person you are.

A binary is a fixed choice; duality is a fluid state. Your opposites may not be the same as mine, and what provides balance for one person might be entirely different for another. For example, some may find balance by shifting between watching TV and reading a book, while others might find their opposite in choosing between watching a show and sleeping. Embracing your duality is about understanding your unique balance, not conforming to a fixed set of opposing characteristics.

When you honor all of who you are, you set a powerful example for others to do the same. This practice deepens your relationships, widens your experiences, and strengthens your confidence. By celebrating all of your authentic selves, you give others permission to do the same. This is a gift you give not only to yourself but to your entire community.

The key to this is understanding that your identity is not a series of mutually exclusive roles, but rather a spectrum of characteristics that you can access freely. You don't have to choose to be just one thing. You have the freedom to be all of it.

The Gift of Presence

Being fully present in each space you occupy, whether it's a group of women, men, elders, children, colleagues, or strangers, is a gift. When you show up authentically, people sense it. They relax and connect with you on a deeper level. They see that you are comfortable with yourself, which gives them permission to be comfortable with you.

You don't have to choose one version of yourself. You can be all of it, and your ability to be present in each facet of your life is a testament to the strength and beauty of your integrated self. This balance is not about perfection; it's about authenticity.

Action Step:

Today, reflect on two seemingly opposite qualities you possess. *How can you honor and express both?* Lean into your duality. Let it make you whole.

That's balance. That's a *MicroVictory*.

Chapter 10
Travel: Expanding Your Mind and Spirit

Travel is one of the most underappreciated forms of personal development. When you leave the familiar and step into new places, cultures, and experiences, you don't just see the world; you see yourself more clearly.

Isolation is failure. Remaining in the same environment, surrounded by the same people, hearing the same perspectives can shrink your worldview and narrow your understanding of life's possibilities. Travel, whether near or far, expands your mind, stretches your empathy, and deepens your appreciation for diversity.

Experience Different Cultures

- Taste foods you've never tried.

- Listen to languages you don't understand.

- Observe customs that challenge your assumptions.

Every time you do, you gain perspective. You realize that the way you grew up, the norms you accepted, and the routines you follow are just one version of life, not the *only* version.

Shift Your Perception

Travel is a powerful tool for releasing judgment and fostering curiosity in the face of criticism. The more you experience different places, people, and cultures, the more you understand that "different" is not "deficient." This profound shift in perspective helps you move past assumptions and embrace a broader view of the world. Even short trips to nearby cities, nature preserves, or new neighborhoods can spark these shifts; you don't have to travel across oceans to broaden your spirit and expand your understanding.

One of the most empowering shifts in perspective is realizing that you are the "CEO of your own life." This doesn't mean you are to blame for everything that happens, but rather that you are responsible for your reactions and choices. This philosophy encourages you to stop blaming external factors and to start taking ownership, recognizing that you have the power to shape your life's direction and outcomes. By embracing this mindset, you foster a sense of empowerment and motivation, consciously choosing a path that aligns with your goals and values to create positive change.

This mindset of personal agency extends to your exposure to newness. Don't wait for adventure to come to you; create it. The act of seeking new experiences is a *MicroVictory* in itself. These small, intentional actions build confidence and expand your world. They can be as simple as booking your first solo trip, trying a new dish, sitting quietly in a new environment to observe, or asking someone about their culture and listening without judgment. Each of these steps is a conscious choice to lead your life with curiosity and purpose, actively creating the experiences that will shape your perspective.

Action Step

This month, plan one new experience. It can be a trip to a new restaurant, a cultural festival, a neighboring town, or a faraway country. Go with an open heart and open mind.

That's exploration. That's a *MicroVictory*.

Chapter 11
Compartmentalize: Redefining Your Relationships

Not all relationships carry the same weight, and that's okay. Understanding the different layers of relationships in your life and managing them intentionally is one of the clearest paths to peace, clarity, and purposeful living.

Why Compartmentalize?

When you clearly understand where each person fits, you:

- Reduce disappointment from misplaced expectations.

- Protect your energy.

- Set healthy boundaries.

- Appreciate people for the role they naturally fit into, without forcing them into more.

It's Not Cold — It's Clarity

Compartmentalization isn't about closing people off or categorizing them with cold detachment. It's about clarity and self-respect.

When you know where people belong in your life, you can:

- Give appropriately.

- Expect reasonably.

- Protect yourself wisely.

Action Step

Today, make a list of the key people in your life. Reflect on where they naturally fit: family, friend, acquaintance, associate, or relative. Adjust your energy, time, and expectations accordingly.

That's discernment. That's a *MicroVictory*.

Chapter 12
Real Life Is Not a Zero-Sum Game

One of the most destructive myths in modern life is the belief that for someone else to succeed, you must fail. The idea that there's a finite amount of opportunity, happiness, and success to go around is a zero-sum game fallacy. When we believe this, we see every promotion, new house, or personal victory for another person as a loss for ourselves. This traps us in a constant state of comparison, fear, and envy. The truth is, another person's success does not diminish your own potential, worth, or happiness. Recognizing this is the first step toward a more fulfilling and connected life.

When you genuinely understand that life is not a zero-sum game, a profound shift happens. You feel lighter, freed from the heavy burden of constant competition. You can celebrate others' victories with authentic joy instead of hidden envy. You become free to walk your own unique path, unburdened by the pressure of comparing your journey to someone else's highlight reel. This shift from a scarcity mindset to an abundance mindset is a fundamental choice that changes how you see and live in the world.

Abundance Over Scarcity

The scarcity mindset is a mental prison built on the assumption of lack. It's the voice that whispers, *"If they got promoted, I'm falling behind,"* or *"If she bought that house, I'll never get mine."* It's the fear that if your friend finds love, there's somehow less left for you. This way of thinking frames life as a competition where resources are limited, and your only option is to protect your small piece of the pie. It creates constant anxiety, turning every interaction into a subtle contest and every achievement into a source of comparison. It leads to a life defined by worry, where you're always looking over your shoulder.

In reality, life is not a pie where every slice taken leaves you with less. Life is more like the sun. Just because someone else is basking in its warmth doesn't mean there's less light for you. The sun shines on everyone. This is the core of the abundance mindset: the belief that there is enough success, happiness, and opportunity for everyone to thrive. This isn't naive optimism; it's a profound truth that frees you to see possibilities instead of limitations. When you embrace abundance, you stop seeing others as rivals and start seeing them as inspiration, as proof that good things are possible and that the world is full of potential.

Your Journey Is Yours

The path to an abundant life begins with focusing on your own journey. A crucial part of this is celebrating others' victories, not as a sign of your own shortcomings, but as a source of motivation. Every time a friend gets a new job or a colleague launches a project, it's evidence that good things are happening. Instead of feeling left behind, you can feel inspired, knowing that opportunities exist and that your own path is unfolding.

It's also essential to recognize that everyone's timing, paths, and desires are different. What's a huge victory for someone else might not even be what you want for your own life. Their success may involve sacrifices or a direction that doesn't align with your personal values. True fulfillment comes not from achieving the same milestones as others, but from building a life that is uniquely yours, one that reflects your deepest values and aspirations.

Your unique version of success—built with intention,

gratitude, and purpose— and fueled by your own *MicroVictories* — is the only scorecard that truly matters.

Community Thrives on Mutual Wins

When you shift from a competitive, scarcity-based mindset to one of collaboration, your relationships become infinitely more rewarding. An abundance mindset allows you to genuinely celebrate others' successes, offer support without jealousy, and work to create shared growth. You are not giving something away; you are creating a positive feedback loop that benefits everyone.

This mindset fosters a community where collaboration and cooperation are the norm. When people believe that success can be shared, they are more likely to work together, mentor each other, and share resources. This not only leads to more opportunities for growth but also reduces the negative emotions of jealousy and envy. In this environment, you'll experience more peace than pressure and more connection than competition. The result is greater happiness and well-being, as you become part of a supportive system that uplifts everyone.

This principle extends to all aspects of life. Sharing knowledge and skills, for instance, doesn't diminish your expertise; it actually deepens your understanding and builds your reputation. Similarly, nurturing strong, supportive relationships creates a positive cycle of well-being and happiness. Innovation and progress often arise from the collaboration of many minds, creating benefits that extend far beyond a single person.

Action Step

This week, intentionally celebrate someone else's success. Compliment their achievement, support their goal, or simply tell them you're proud of them.

That's generosity of spirit. That's a *MicroVictory*.

Chapter 13
Reciprocity: The Balance of Giving and Receiving

Relationships flourish when there's a healthy, natural exchange, a flow of giving and receiving that feels effortless and mutually beneficial. True connection isn't built on obligation or manipulation; it's founded on reciprocity.

This isn't a cold, calculated transaction, but a living, breathing dynamic where both people feel genuinely seen, heard, and valued. It's the constant, unspoken agreement that both partners are willing to meet each other's needs and invest emotionally.

Without this fundamental balance, even the most promising relationships can wither, leaving one or both individuals feeling drained and unappreciated. Reciprocity is the secret to moving beyond simply existing together and into a space of shared well-being and lasting connection.

The Anatomy of Caring: Caring Requires Action

Kindness is a feeling. Caring is an action. You can feel empathy, compassion, or fondness toward someone, but without effort, those feelings mean little. Genuine relationships require more than internal sentiment; they need outward expression. This is where reciprocity begins. It's the tangible effort we put in to show that someone matters. It's the choice to:

- *Call back:* To close the communication loop and show you heard them.

- *Show up:* To be there in moments of celebration and

moments of crisis.

- *Lend a hand:* To offer practical support, like helping them move or watching their children.

- *Offer time, attention, and intention:* To put away your phone and truly listen, giving them your most precious, non-renewable resource: **your focus.**

These actions are the building blocks of a reciprocal relationship. They are the non-verbal gifts we give, proving that our feelings of care are real and actionable. A relationship where one person feels and the other acts is destined for imbalance.

The Give-and-Take of Connection: Transactions Aren't Bad

It's easy to bristle at the word "transaction," but hear me out. A transaction simply means an exchange. And in every relationship, even friendships, there is a transaction, a gift for a get. That's not cold; that's real. This isn't about keeping a strict, running tally of who did what, but about a natural flow where contributions are exchanged and valued.

You give love, you hope to receive love: This is the emotional core of a relationship. You offer affection, support, and acceptance, and in turn, you want to feel that same warmth and security.

You offer trust, you expect trustworthiness: When you make yourself vulnerable, you expect your partner to guard that vulnerability with respect and honesty.

You invest time, you desire companionship: You choose to spend your moments with someone, not for a quid pro quo, but for the shared experience of connection, laughter, and support that time together creates.

This healthy exchange is what allows a relationship to grow. When both partners feel they are contributing and receiving fairly, the relationship becomes a source of energy, not a drain.

The Three Types of Reciprocity

Reciprocity isn't a one-size-fits-all concept. It manifests in different ways, and understanding these forms can help us better navigate our relationships.

- *Generalized Reciprocity:* This is the most selfless form, where you give without expecting a specific return from the person you've helped. It's the kindness you show a stranger, the favor you do for a friend, just because you can. This form of giving builds a sense of community and trust on a broader scale, creating a positive, communal feedback loop.

- *Balanced Reciprocity:* This is the ideal in a close relationship. It's an equal give-and-take, where both partners feel they are contributing and receiving fairly. This doesn't mean you're always doing the same exact thing for each other. One partner might be the primary emotional support, while the other provides practical support. The key is that both feel the exchange is equitable and fulfilling.

- *Negative Reciprocity:* This is an imbalanced, unhealthy form of exchange. In this dynamic, one partner feels used, taken advantage of, or drained. It's a one-way street where one person is consistently giving while the other is consistently taking. This dynamic erodes trust and can lead to burnout, resentment, and a breakdown of the relationship.

Be the Friend You'd Want: The Blueprint for Healthy Relationships

A reciprocal relationship starts with you. The qualities you value in others are the same ones you should cultivate in yourself. When you consistently act with intention and generosity, you attract relationships of a similar caliber. The key is *balance*: not overextending yourself or under-contributing. By embodying the following traits, you not only improve your existing relationships but also set the standard for the new ones you bring into your life.

- *Trustworthy:* Reliability and integrity are the cornerstones of trust. Be the person who follows through on their promises.

- *Reliable:* Show up when you say you will, and be the person your loved ones can count on.

- *Present:* Put away distractions and give people your full attention. This is a powerful way to show you value them.

- *Attentive:* Pay attention to the details of their lives. Remember important dates, ask about their struggles, and celebrate their small wins.

- *Supportive:* Be their biggest fan, offering encouragement and a listening ear without judgment.

These traits are the hallmarks of a healthy, reciprocal relationship. When both partners are committed to being their best selves, the relationship becomes a powerful force for mutual growth and well-being.

Guard Against Exploitation

A reciprocal relationship feels like a gentle back-and-forth, where no one feels drained, and everyone feels valued. It's not about keeping a running tally of who did what, but about a general sense of balance. However, awareness is crucial. If you constantly find yourself giving without receiving, you might be in a relationship built on negative reciprocity. Over time, this imbalance erodes the foundation of the relationship and can leave you feeling taken advantage of, unappreciated, and ultimately burned out.

Reciprocity does not mean keeping score. But it does mean awareness.

It's important to pay attention to the subtle cues:

- *Do you feel energized after spending time with this person, or do you feel drained?*

- *Do they ask you about your life, or is the conversation always focused on them?*

- *Are they there for you in your moments of need, or do you always have to be the one offering support?*

A healthy relationship should feel like a safe and supportive space, not a constant effort to keep someone else afloat.

Why Reciprocity Is Essential

The presence of reciprocity is a cornerstone of a healthy life, not just a healthy relationship. It is a powerful force for well-being, promoting emotional health and preventing burnout.

- *Builds Trust and Commitment:* When both partners consistently invest in the relationship, it fosters a deep sense of trust and security. You know you can rely on this person, which makes it safe to be vulnerable and authentic. This trust is the glue that holds a long-lasting relationship together.

- *Promotes Emotional Well-being:* Feeling seen, heard, and valued is fundamental to our emotional health and happiness. A reciprocal relationship provides a sense of belonging and connection, which are essential for navigating life's challenges.

- *Prevents Burnout:* In relationships that lack reciprocity, one partner may feel used and unappreciated, ultimately leading to burnout. This can lead to resentment, emotional exhaustion, and even physical health issues. A balanced give-and-take protects both individuals from the negative effects of a one-sided dynamic.

Navigating Low-Reciprocity Relationships

If you find yourself in a relationship that lacks reciprocity, it's not a lost cause, but it requires intentional action.

- *Communicate Your Needs:* The first step is to openly and honestly express your needs and expectations. Use "I" statements to share how the imbalance makes you feel without placing blame. For example, *"I feel unappreciated when I'm the only one initiating plans."* This opens the door for a conversation rather than an accusation.

- *Practice Self-Love:* In the meantime, focus on nurturing yourself and meeting your own needs. Lean on other supportive relationships and engage in activities that bring you joy and a sense of purpose. This isn't selfish; it's a form of self-preservation that prevents you from becoming completely drained.

- *Seek Outside Help:* A couples counselor or therapist can provide a safe space to facilitate communication and address imbalances. A professional can help both partners understand their roles in the dynamic and develop strategies for creating a healthier exchange.

- *Re-evaluate the Relationship:* If you have made genuine efforts to communicate and create change, but the imbalance persists, it may be time to re-evaluate the relationship dynamic. You deserve to be in relationships where you feel valued and supported, and sometimes the healthiest choice is to walk away from a dynamic that is consistently taking more than it gives.

Reciprocity is the very essence of a vibrant, healthy relationship. By understanding its components and practicing its principles, you can cultivate connections that are not only deeply rewarding but also a powerful source of growth and happiness for everyone involved.

Action Step

Reflect on a current relationship. Ask: *"Am I contributing meaningfully? Am I receiving meaningfully?"*

If there's an imbalance, communicate and adjust with kindness.

That's clarity. That's a *MicroVictory.*

Chapter 14
Master Your Smile: The Language of Presence

A smile is one of the simplest yet most powerful tools for celebrating your *MicroVictories*. It is more than a reflex or a fleeting expression; it is a form of language, one that transcends culture, geography, and background. A smile says, without words, *I am okay. I am here. I am present with intention.* When you choose to smile, you are practicing a *MicroVictory* — the shift from autopilot to awareness, from annoyance to appreciation.

Too often, we underestimate the impact of something so small. Yet a smile can change the energy of a room. It can alter your mood. It can soften the hardest moments. It is one of the most accessible and immediate ways to ground yourself in gratitude, celebrate the now, and broadcast contentment to the world around you.

Your Smile Is Yours

A smile is deeply personal. It belongs first and foremost to you. Sometimes, it functions like clothing, a shroud covering what's hidden underneath: emotional pain, weariness, or even despair. At other times, it serves as armor, not to hide, but to project strength, resolve, and determination. Both are valid. A smile doesn't have to mean you're without struggle. It can mean you've chosen to carry yourself with resilience in the midst of it.

But here's the truth: a forced smile rarely works. People can tell. Just as a genuine smile radiates warmth, an insincere one creates distance. The most powerful smiles are not exaggerated or theatrical.

They are subtle: the gentle curve of lips when you're at peace, the softening of eyes when you feel safe, the quiet expression of gratitude. These are the smiles that resonate. These are the smiles that strengthen presence.

A Smile Is Self-Serving, and That's Okay

Smiling benefits you first, and that is not selfish. Studies show that smiling can lower stress, reduce blood pressure, and even elevate mood. The act itself sends signals to the brain that you are safe, content, and capable. This shift in chemistry primes you to seek joy and recognize moments of gratitude more easily.

But the ripple doesn't stop there. Your smile influences others, too. It can break the tension in a room, soften a difficult conversation, or serve as an unspoken invitation to connect. Smiling creates resonance. Just as one candle can light another without losing its flame, one smile can multiply into dozens. The people around you feel your presence differently when you carry it with calm confidence and warmth.

The Snapshot of Happiness

Think of a smile as a snapshot — a moment captured in real time. It doesn't have to be grand, wide, or gleaming. The best smiles often come in small doses:

- The faint grin when you notice the morning sun through your window.

- The subtle upturn when you complete a task you've been putting off.

- The relaxed curve of contentment when you're surrounded by people who make you feel safe.

These little snapshots of happiness are proof of presence. They remind you that joy does not always come in sweeping gestures; sometimes, it is found in the tiniest flicker of gratitude expressed on your face.

Smile With Intention

Like everything else in this book — celebration, gratitude, purpose, and connection — a smile is most powerful when it is deliberate. Smile because you mean it, not because someone expects it from you. Smile because you're grateful to wake up in the morning, because you've honored a small promise to yourself, or because you're witnessing beauty in the ordinary.

When you smile with intention, it becomes more than an expression. It becomes a *MicroVictory*. It says: *I chose gratitude in this moment. I chose presence. I chose peace.*

My Smile, My Story

Over the years, people have often complimented me on my smile. It's one of the things I've shared most naturally, even in difficult situations. I've smiled with people who were in despair, not to minimize their pain, but to shine a light and show them that there is always hope, that the tunnel does, in fact, have an end.

But the truth is, I don't smile for others first. I smile because I am constantly reflecting on my life, the experiences I've had, and the gratitude I feel for them. My smile is a reflection of my contentment, of knowing that I do my best whenever I can. It is a reminder to myself as much as it is a gift to others.

For me, smiling is not a performance. It is practice. It is a way of choosing presence, gratitude, and peace over frustration, negativity, or disconnection. And when others see that smile, it has the power to lift them, too. That's the beauty of it: what begins as a *MicroVictory* inside you becomes an act of service to others.

Action Step

Throughout your day, notice when you smile naturally. Reflect on what sparked it — *contentment, gratitude, connection?*

Make a mental note of those moments. Cultivate more of them.

That's awareness. That's a *MicroVictory*.

Chapter 15
The Intentional Beat: Integrating the Festival High

The air doesn't just carry sound—it vibrates with it. Stand in the center of a massive festival crowd and you'll notice something subtle but undeniable: the bass is no longer something you hear. It's something you *feel*, something that seems to move through you, reorganizing your very sense of self.

There is a kind of magic here that cannot be reduced or replicated in isolation. Thousands of strangers, breathing in rhythm, moving in sync, surrendering to the same pulse. For a moment, individuality softens, and something collective takes its place.

This is not an accident. It is a state you can learn to understand—and more importantly, to carry with you.

The Anatomy of the High

What you experience at a festival may feel spiritual, but it is also deeply biological.

Music, especially in a live setting, acts as a direct pathway into the brain's reward system. When the beat drops, when a melody crests, when anticipation resolves into release, your brain responds instantly. Dopamine floods your system, creating pleasure, motivation, and emotional intensity. Alongside it, oxytocin—the hormone responsible for bonding and trust—begins to rise.

This combination does more than make you feel good. It connects you.

What emerges is a phenomenon known as *collective effervescence*: a shared emotional state where the boundary between self and group begins to blur. You are no longer just witnessing the experience—you are participating in something larger than yourself.

In a world that often isolates, the festival becomes a rare and powerful ritual of belonging.

Frisson: When the Body Says Yes

There are moments in music that seem to bypass thought entirely.

A sudden key change. A voice that stretches just beyond what feels possible. A drop that arrives after perfect tension. And then—without warning—a chill moves down your spine, your skin tingles, your arms rise in goosebumps.

This is frisson.

It is your nervous system responding to beauty, surprise, and emotional significance all at once. It happens when expectation meets transcendence—when something is not just heard, but *felt as meaningful.*

Not everyone experiences frisson in the same way, but for those who do, it becomes a signal: a reminder that you are open, receptive, and fully engaged with the moment.

In a sense, it is your body confirming what your mind cannot yet articulate:

this matters.

The Raver's North Star: PLUR

Amid the chaos, the lights, and the overwhelming sensory input, there exists a simple philosophy that grounds the entire experience: **PLUR**.

- **Peace** — choosing calm over conflict
- **Love** — offering empathy and shared joy
- **Unity** — recognizing that, for this moment, we are one
- **Respect** — honoring yourself, others, and the space you occupy

PLUR is more than a slogan. It is a decision about how you show up.

It is expressed in small gestures—a smile, a helping hand, a moment of patience in a dense crowd. It is reinforced through rituals, like the exchange of beaded bracelets, where two strangers briefly step into a shared rhythm of trust and acknowledgment.

These interactions may be fleeting, but their impact is not. They reveal something essential: connection does not require history. It requires presence.

Gratitude and Intention: The Mental Scaffolding

The peak moments—the drops, the lights, the emotional surges—are powerful, but they are not what sustain the experience. What gives the festival its lasting impact is something quieter: intention.

When you arrive with the intention to be present, everything shifts. You are no longer chasing the next high or consuming the experience as it unfolds. Instead, you begin to participate in shaping it.

A simple intention—*to be someone others feel safe around*—changes your posture, your awareness, your interactions. You become attuned not just to your own experience, but to the collective one.

Gratitude deepens this shift.

When you take a moment to acknowledge the artists, the crew, the strangers around you, and the circumstances that brought you here, you ground the intensity of the moment. Gratitude transforms a fleeting surge of pleasure into something more stable: contentment.

It anchors you.

Action Step: Anchor the Feeling

Before you leave your next deeply positive experience—whether it's a festival, a concert, or even a meaningful conversation—pause.

Take 10 seconds.

Breathe in slowly, and ask yourself: *What am I feeling right now?* Then ask: *How did I contribute to this feeling?*

Name it. Claim it. Let it register.

This simple act creates a mental imprint. It teaches your brain that the feeling is not random—it is something you can access again, intentionally.

Carrying the Beat Forward

The challenge is not experiencing the festival. The challenge is leaving it.

When the music fades and the lights disappear, the contrast can feel sharp. The world seems quieter, less connected, more fragmented. It is tempting to believe that what you felt was temporary—something tied to a place, a crowd, or a sound system.

But that belief is incomplete.

What you experienced was not created by the festival. The festival revealed what is already available to you.

The openness.

The connection.

The capacity for joy, empathy, and presence.

These are not environmental conditions—they are internal ones.

The beat does not disappear when the music stops. It becomes subtler. It moves inward. And if you listen closely, you will find it again—in conversation, in stillness, in the smallest shared moments of everyday life.

"We don't go to festivals to escape life, but so that life doesn't escape us."

In that field, under those towering speakers, something essential becomes clear. The roles you carry—the titles, the responsibilities, the identities—fall away.

What remains is simple and profound:

You are a heartbeat in a sea of heartbeats, perfectly in time.

And when you choose to carry that rhythm into an ordinary moment—on a sidewalk, in a conversation, in a single conscious breath—that's a microvictory.

Chapter 16
The Rule of 3s: Redefining Taste Through Exposure

We've all heard someone say, *"I don't like country music,"* or *"I can't get into anime,"* or *"Reality TV just isn't for me."* And maybe you've said something similar. But the truth is, it's not always about dislike. It's often about unfamiliarity.

Enter the **"Rule of 3s."**

The rule of 3s is simple: Before you dismiss an entire genre, subject, or experience, you must engage with at least three examples of it.

That's it. Three songs. Three shows. Three movies. Three dishes. Three books. Three episodes. Three tries.

They don't have to be random either. Choose three pieces from one artist, director, culture, language, or platform. Find what others love and give it an honest try. You don't have to become a superfan; you just have to explore.

Taste Requires Curiosity

Disliking something after thoughtful exposure is valid. But disliking something because of a single experience (or worse, a stereotype) robs you of growth. Taste is developed, not inherited. It evolves through exposure, openness, and curiosity.

The Rule of 3s in Practice

- Don't like jazz? Listen to three different artists from three different eras.

- Think you're not into foreign films? Try three from different countries or directors.

- Feel like poetry isn't your thing? Read three poems by three different poets.

You may walk away still feeling the same, and that's fine. But often, you'll find something that resonates. One line. One scene. One sound. And that moment is a *MicroVictory*.

A Story From the Field

In college, I was a new member educator, pledge master, and grandmaster of ceremonies for my fraternity, Kappa Sigma. I taught and mentored dozens of young men in both academic and social pursuits — guys from a wide range of socioeconomic and geographic backgrounds.

A lot of them weren't fans of hip hop/rap, country music, or EDM. But I challenged them with the Rule of 3s. I told them: *Find three songs in that genre that you like — enough to sing along with the chorus.*

That was enough to open their minds, spark interest, and engage them in conversations they otherwise would've opted out of. It built bridges. It sparked friendships. And more often than not, it expanded their musical taste.

How to Talk About What's Not Your Style

After you've applied the Rule of 3s, you can say with confidence:

- *"I've tried a few, I'm just not into it — yet."*

- *"I'm new to the genre, still learning."*

- *"It's not really my style, but I respect it."*

No need for defensiveness. No need for judgment. Just honesty and openness.

Action Step

Pick something you've written off in the past — a genre, art form, activity, or food. Find three versions of it. Give them a fair try.

For example:

<u>*Rule of Threes – Example Subjects / Topics*</u>

- *Reality TV shows*
- *Country music songs*
- *Intriguing architectural styles*
- *Regional noodle dishes*
- *Local cultural rituals*
- *Classic folk songs*
- *Sweet white wines*
- *Guilty pleasure podcasts*
- *Local coffee shops*
- *Walkable European cities*
- *Vintage horror movies*
- *Theme park snacks*
- *Night market foods*
- *Indie music discoveries*
- *Everyday science wonders*
- *Acoustic guitar songs*
- *Seasonal world festivals*
- *Vinyl record collectibles*
- *Signature home recipes*

MicroVictories

- *Solo travel hacks*
- *Midcentury modern furniture*
- *Subtitled anime series*
- *Childhood comfort snacks*
- *Accidental scientific discoveries*

That's exploration. That's humility. That's a *MicroVictory*.

Chapter 17
Build Your Role Model

We're taught to look up to people — celebrities, athletes, public figures, even family members — as role models. But more often than not, those figures are presented to us as *whole packages.* We're expected to admire them entirely, as if a single person can fully embody everything we aspire to become.

That's a mistake.

A true role model isn't a singular person. It's a collection. A mosaic of characteristics drawn from a variety of people, real or imagined, living or gone. When you build your role model piece by piece, you allow for nuance, flexibility, and strength that no one individual could ever provide.

I've never had one role model. Instead, I've built a personal composite of traits I admire and try to embody. I admire my mother's resilience. My father's tireless work ethic. Neil deGrasse Tyson and Bad Bunny's charisma and perspective. Dirk Nowitzki's fluid jump shot. John Legend's smooth, expressive voice. Alexandra Daddario's piercing eyes. Justin Gatlin and Tyson Gay's blazing speed. Pedro Pascal's empathetic masculinity. The capybara's patience and demeanor.

Each of these beings brings something uniquely inspiring to the table, and none of them is perfect.

Take the Pressure Off the Pedestal

When you idolize one individual as your role model, you set yourself up for disillusionment. People are people. They are fallible, flawed, and capable of making poor decisions. The higher the pedestal, the longer the fall. And when that fall comes, as it often does, it can leave you feeling betrayed, confused, and disconnected.

When your role model is a concept instead of a person, your foundation is much stronger. Instead of tying your values and goals to one human, you anchor them in a range of qualities that you can carry forward.

- You can admire someone's discipline without adopting their worldview.

- You can learn from someone's success without excusing their failures.

- You can love someone's art without modeling your life after theirs.

Build With Intention

Start paying attention to the traits that stir something in you:

- *Who makes you want to move with more purpose?*

- *Whose communication style makes you feel heard?*

- *Whose physicality motivates you to take care of your body?*

- *Who models grace under pressure?*

- *Who shows vulnerability with strength?*

Write these names down. Beside each one, write the trait you admire. Then ask yourself: *What does this look like in me? What would it take to embody this trait in my own way?*

When you intentionally build your role model, you start to construct a blueprint, not of who you want to be, but of the kind of energy you want to live with.

Avoid the Idol Trap

Idolatry places unrealistic expectations on people. When they inevitably fall short, we're left disappointed or even devastated. But when you admire traits, not titles — when you honor characteristics over characters — you avoid the trap entirely.

Instead of saying, *"I want to be like 'him' or 'her,'"* say, *"I want to develop 'that' quality."*

This mindset empowers you. It puts the focus on development, not duplication. It makes your growth personal and grounded.

Become the Blueprint

Over time, the role model you build becomes a mirror, not just a reflection of what you admire, but a guide for who you are becoming.

You can mix resilience, creativity, grace, humor, logic, patience, and boldness — in **your** way, with **your** voice, in **your** time. That's how you move from admiration to embodiment.

You don't need to be perfect. You need to be consistent. You need to be curious. You need to be willing to evolve.

Let the people who inspire you serve as signposts, not destinations.

Action Step

Create your *Role Model Map*. Write down 5–10 people (famous or not, real or fictional) and the one trait from each that you admire most. Then reflect on how you can begin embodying each of those qualities in your own life.

That's personal power. That's intentional growth. That's a *MicroVictory*.

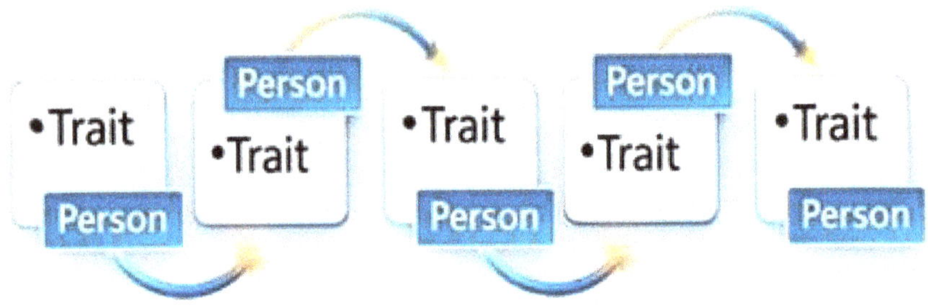

Chapter 18
Be Selfishly Kind: The Win-Win Philosophy of Good Deeds

We often grow up being told that kindness must be selfless, that the moment we gain something from helping others, it somehow loses its purity. But what if that's not true? What if the most sustainable, honest form of kindness isn't selfless at all, but selfishly kind?

Being selfishly kind means doing good for others while also recognizing that doing so benefits you in some way — emotionally, spiritually, or even practically. It's about merging generosity with self-awareness. When you act from this space, kindness becomes a joy, not a burden. It's no longer about sacrifice or martyrdom; it's about intentional giving that uplifts both you and the person you're helping.

The Power of Intentional Kindness

When you do something kind like hold a door, listen without judgment, pay for someone's coffee, or help a friend move, there's almost always a small cost: your time, energy, or attention. But the act feels easier when you consciously acknowledge the reward that comes with it. Maybe the benefit is seeing someone smile. Maybe it's the quiet satisfaction of knowing you made a tough day lighter for someone who needed it.

The benefit doesn't have to be material. It can be emotional, spiritual, or even subconscious. A sense of pride, fulfillment, or peace — these are valid rewards. When you view good deeds as mutually beneficial exchanges, kindness stops feeling like a sacrifice and starts feeling like empowerment.

Doing Good with a Return

Here's the truth: we all want to feel useful, appreciated, and connected. When you're selfishly kind, you're not manipulating people or giving with strings attached; you're simply aware that positivity creates momentum.

Maybe the benefit is small:

- You feel lighter after brightening someone's day.

- You strengthen a bond with someone who'll remember your kindness.

- You open a door that leads to unexpected opportunities or friendships.

- You plant a seed of gratitude that might grow into future generosity — theirs or yours.

And yes, sometimes the benefit might be tangible. Maybe the person you helped buys you a drink later, covers your meal, recommends you for a job, or simply sings your praises to someone else. There's nothing wrong with that. Gratitude has a way of coming full circle, and when you act with integrity and intention, that circle benefits everyone involved.

The Keys Story

A great example of this happened recently when I went to an EDM concert at a local venue with a friend. Everyone was dancing and enjoying themselves when I noticed a set of car keys on a lanyard lying on the ground. No one around seemed to notice them, so I started asking people nearby if they had dropped their keys. No one claimed them, so I picked them up and began walking toward the host stand, asking people along the way if they were missing their keys.

When I turned them in and made my way back to my friend in the crowd, a group of guys appeared — one of them clearly searching the floor. He went to the stand, retrieved his keys, and then came back through the crowd to find me. He thanked me and, as a token of appreciation, handed me a mini bottle of Fireball.

I had no way of knowing he'd do that — though, in truth, people at concerts tend to be generous when you help them. But that wasn't why I did it.

So, did I do the right thing by trying to find the owner? Yes.

Did asking random strangers allow me to engage with new people in a positive, non-threatening way? Yes.

Did I turn in the keys out of the goodness of my heart? Yes.

Did I also recognize that there was a chance the person would be grateful and reward the good deed? Absolutely.

That's the essence of being selfishly kind — acting out of kindness while acknowledging that doing so may bring a positive return. I didn't do it for the Fireball, but I also didn't deny that part of me understood the possibility of gratitude. The act itself was rooted in goodness, but the awareness of potential reward made it even sweeter.

The Inconvenient Gift

True generosity often involves inconvenience. It's staying an extra 15 minutes to help a coworker finish a task, giving a friend a ride when it's out of your way, or offering encouragement when you're tired yourself. These moments stretch you, and that's where the growth happens.

But being selfishly kind reframes inconvenience. You don't focus on what you lose; you focus on what you gain: perspective, purpose, connection, or peace of mind. When you choose to be helpful with awareness, even a small sacrifice feels meaningful because you know there's a reason behind it. You're not just reacting; you're creating an intentional moment of goodness that reflects your values.

The Emotional ROI

Think of kindness like emotional investing. You give your time, effort, or attention knowing it will pay dividends in joy, reputation, and self-respect. Each act compounds, reinforcing who you are and how you move through the world.

When you are selfishly kind, you:

- Strengthen your emotional intelligence.

- Build a reputation of reliability and warmth.

- Create a positive self-image rooted in purpose.

- Develop gratitude by recognizing your capacity to help.

You are training your mind to look for goodness, to seek meaning in the exchange. Every time you find even a small benefit — a smile, a thank-you, a brief connection — you reinforce that doing good feels good. That's not selfish. That's sustainable.

Redefining Selfishness

We often treat "selfish" as a dirty word, but not all forms of self-interest are negative. There's a difference between being selfish at the expense of others and being selfish in alignment with them. Selfishly nice people don't take; they share. They give with awareness and receive with gratitude.

When you act from this mindset, every interaction becomes an opportunity to create mutual benefit. You're no longer drained by helping others because you've recognized the reward within it. You're filling your own cup while pouring into someone else's.

The Always-Good Deed

If you always look for the potential benefit, even a tiny one, then no matter what you do, it becomes a good deed. You've already won. Either someone else feels better, or you do. Often, both.

Smile at someone on a bad day. Offer help without being asked. Lend your time, share your knowledge, or give encouragement freely, not because you have to, but because you want to, knowing there's something in it for everyone involved.

That benefit might be as simple as knowing you made a difference. It might be seeing gratitude light up someone's face. Or it might be the quiet satisfaction of aligning your actions with your values, of knowing that in a world often ruled by indifference, you chose connection.

That's the beauty of being selfishly kind: it guarantees that kindness will always have value. You don't have to choose between giving and gaining. You can do both. And when you do, kindness stops being random; it becomes intentional, powerful, and deeply human.

Action Step: Practice Selfish Kindness

This week, commit to one act of "selfish" kindness each day

— something that genuinely helps another person while also offering you a benefit, however small.

- Help someone with a task because it feels good to be useful.

- Compliment a stranger and notice how it lifts your energy too.

- Give your time to someone in need and observe how that deepens your gratitude.

At the end of each day, reflect on your act and ask yourself:

What did I gain from helping today?

Train your brain to recognize the reward in giving. When you find meaning in every good deed, kindness becomes effortless, not an obligation, but a natural extension of who you are.

And when you recognize the joy that comes from even the smallest act of intentional kindness — that moment of warmth, connection, or gratitude — you've already achieved what this book is all about.

That's a *MicroVictory*.

Conclusion
The Celebration Continues

Life is a collection of moments — not all grand, not all easy, but all meaningful when seen through the right lens. *MicroVictories* remind us that happiness isn't something we chase; it's something we create through intention, gratitude, and purpose. Every smile, every act of kindness, every moment of presence is a small win; proof that progress doesn't always roar; sometimes it whispers.

You've learned to celebrate the small things, to be grateful for what already exists, and to act with purpose in relationships, community, and self. You've discovered that abundance is not about having more but about being more — more aware, more giving, more connected.

Each day offers opportunities to build joy through conscious action. Whether you're mastering your smile, being selfishly nice, or simply noticing a moment of peace amid chaos, remember: you are growing. You are winning.

Celebrate your small wins. Honor your progress. Continue to live with intention and gratitude. Because when you do, even the smallest acts become the greatest triumphs.

Every day you choose awareness, that's a *MicroVictory*.

Appendix
100 MicroVictories: The Small, Everyday Wins Worth Celebrating

Here are 100 *MicroVictories* — the small, everyday wins worth celebrating:

1. Waking up on time.

2. Waking up before your alarm goes off.

3. Getting out of bed without hitting snooze.

4. Making your bed.

5. Drinking a full glass of water after waking up.

6. Brushing your teeth for a full two minutes.

7. Flossing.

8. Washing your face.

9. Putting on deodorant.

10. Choosing an outfit without changing three times.

11. Packing lunch instead of buying it.

12. Eating breakfast at home.

13. Feeding your pet on time.

14. Taking your vitamins or medication.

15. Charging your phone overnight.

16. Leaving the house with everything you need.

17. Grabbing your keys on the first try.

18. Not forgetting your water bottle.

19. Catching all green lights on your commute.

20. Getting to work without using GPS.

21. Parking without needing to reverse and adjust.

22. Arriving early.

23. Remembering a birthday.

24. Remembering a co-worker's birthday.

25. Holding the door open for someone.

26. Receiving a smile from a stranger.

27. Giving a compliment.

28. Receiving a compliment.

29. Finishing a cup of coffee before it gets cold.

30. Drinking water throughout the day.

31. Replying to an email right away.

32. Deleting unnecessary emails.

33. Emptying your inbox.

34. Making a to-do list.

35. Checking something off your to-do list.

36. Taking the stairs instead of the elevator.

37. Not skipping lunch.

38. Eating something healthy.

39. Saying no to junk food.

40. Going for a short walk.

41. Standing up to stretch during a break.

42. Not checking social media during a meeting.

43. Returning a text message.

44. Calling someone back.

45. Not losing your pen.

46. Refilling your water bottle.

47. Completing a task before the deadline.

48. Saying "thank you" with intention.

49. Staying calm during a frustrating moment.

50. Reframing a negative thought.

51. Writing something down before you forget.

52. Fixing a typo before sending.

53. Laughing at something unexpected.

54. Making someone else laugh.

55. Remembering someone's name.

56. Not interrupting during a conversation.

57. Letting someone merge in traffic.

58. Yielding the right of way without getting annoyed.

59. Finding a clean bathroom when you need one.

60. Getting exact change.

61. Picking up something someone dropped.

62. Helping someone carry something heavy.

63. Bringing your reusable bag to the store.

64. Not forgetting your grocery list.

65. Finding everything on your list.

66. Staying within your budget.

67. Cooking a meal at home.

68. Cleaning up immediately after.

69. Running the dishwasher.

70. Emptying the dishwasher.

71. Taking out the trash without being asked.

72. Doing a load of laundry.

73. Folding the laundry.

74. Putting away the laundry.

75. Watering your plants.

76. Feeding your pet on time again.

77. Playing with your pet.

78. Picking up a piece of trash on the sidewalk.

79. Recycling properly.

80. Turning off unused lights.

81. Lowering the thermostat when you leave.

82. Finding a parking spot close to the entrance.

83. Remembering an appointment without a reminder.

84. Writing down an idea before it disappears.

85. Finishing a book chapter.

86. Reading instead of scrolling.

87. Watching an episode and not bingeing.

88. Putting your phone down for 30 minutes.

89. Going to bed on time.

90. Charging your devices before bed

91. Setting your alarm without stress.

92. Preparing your clothes for tomorrow.

93. Prepping breakfast or lunch ahead of time.

94. Journaling a thought or reflection.

95. Brushing and flossing before bed.

96. Washing your face again at night.

97. Choosing to breathe instead of react.

98. Saying "I love you" or "I appreciate you."

99. Forgiving yourself for something small.

100. Going to sleep knowing you tried your best.

Acknowledgment

This book is the culmination of a lifetime of small moments, lessons learned, and gratitude earned through experience.

To my parents — thank you for your resilience, work ethic, love, and example. Your values shaped who I am and laid the foundation for the principles in this book.

To my mentors — thank you for your guidance, perspective, and belief. Your lessons, both spoken and lived, helped shape my growth and sense of purpose.

To the gentlemen of La Salle College High School and my fraternity brothers of Kappa Sigma Fraternity, Rho Beta Chapter at St. John's University, Queens — thank you for the brotherhood, accountability, and shared experiences that taught me the importance of community and responsibility.

To my friends and family — thank you for the connection, support, and encouragement that inspired many of these pages.

Every relationship played a role in these pages. Thank you for being part of my MicroVictories.